VOTES FOR WOMEN: A 75TH ANNIVERSARY ALBUM

by
Ellen DuBois
Professor of History, University of California, Los Angeles

Karen Kearns
Curator of Western History, Huntington Library

with an introduction by

Anne Firor Scott
Professor Emeritus, Duke University

HUNTINGTON LIBRARY
San Marino, California

This publication is made possible in part through the generosity of Helen and Peter Bing.

FRONT COVER: Postcard from the 1911 California campaign.

BACK COVER: Catching Up With China: This beautiful banner, carried in the 1912 New York City suffrage parade by national suffrage president, Anna Howard Shaw, honors the international character of the woman suffrage movement. In 1911 in a provincial revolution, militant women in Nanking, China, inspired by sister "suffragettes" from England, temporarily won the right to vote in Parliamentary elections.

ISBN 0-87328-157-8

Acknowledgements

This publication commemorates the 75th anniversary of the passage of the Nineteenth Amendment to the U.S. Constitution. It was produced in conjunction with an exhibition called "Votes for Women: A 75th Anniversary Celebration," displayed at the Huntington Library from October 1995 to January 1996.

The two people crucial to the exhibit are the late William Moffett and Helen Bing. Bill saw the importance of this subject and did everything possible to make the exhibit happen. That he was not with us to see it is a profound sadness for everyone involved. Helen Bing's quick and enthusiastic support for this project was a wonderful gift and has been absolutely fundamental to the realization of Votes for Women.

We hope to have met her generous ambitions and high standards in the exhibit and this publication. The entire Huntington staff has been enormously helpful and a few individuals deserve special mention: Peggy Spear, who believed in the project from the very first; Robert Ritchie, who steadfastly stood behind the exhibit; Virginia Renner, who has watched over women's history at the Library for a long time; Mary Robertson; Erika Erickson; Peggy Park Bernal; Avelina Moeller; Jennie Watts; Cathy Cherbosque; and others too numerous to mention.

Rob Ball designed a beautiful and exciting exhibit that captured the spirit of the suffrage movement.

Thanks especially to the wonderful advisory committee. Putting together this exhibit gave us all a little taste of how generations of women in the suffrage movement worked together and created something of which they could be proud.

Votes for Women Advisory Council

Lois Banner, Professor, USC Department of History
Martha Banta, Professor, UCLA Department of English
Helen Bing, Community Leader
Louise Cook, Vice President Agent Development, Prudential Preferred Properties
Susan Grimes, President, Los Angeles City Commission on the Status of Women
Jeanne Holt, Head, Mayfield Senior School, Pasadena
Bea Mandel, Community Leader, UCLA Alumni Association
Jean Stone, Author
Reva Tooley, Community Leader

Introduction by Anne Firor Scott

The items described in this publication are drawn from the remarkable collections of the Huntington Library. Behind each item, any student of woman suffrage will see whole stories. For people new to the subject, the same objects will provide views of this extraordinary social movement which after years and years of work led in 1920 to the enfranchisement of American women, or at least of white women.

It would be possible to look back even further, to Margaret Brent in the seventeenth century demanding a vote in the Maryland Assembly, to Hannah Corbin Lee in eighteenth-century Virginia asking why she, a taxpayer, was not permitted to vote, to other individuals here and there through all the years before 1848. But in 1848 came the first formal demand for woman suffrage from a substantial number of women and men.

In that year, an almost casually summoned meeting launched what would become a formidable social movement. Read carefully the proceedings of the Seneca Falls Convention. Virtually the whole agenda of the "woman movement," as it was called, is laid out there, and some of the aims are still unrealized.

Then read the speeches and letters of people like Susan B. Anthony and Lucy Stone of the first generation of identified suffragists, the proceedings of the American Equal Rights Association, the letters of other suffragists, especially those in the West.

Observe the movement incorporating some black women, like Sojourner Truth. Later, younger black women would feel excluded and would form their own suffrage organizations. Notice the development of organizations of wage-earning women and observe the split when brash young women, like Alice Paul and Lucy Burns, challenged the leaders of the National American Woman Suffrage Association and formed their own Woman's Party. The question comes, was the division harmful or did the competition lead to more accomplishment?

Indeed, open to almost any page, trace out the meaning of the artifact you are seeing, and there you are in the midst of one of the most significant social-political movements of the nineteenth and early twentieth centuries.

Co-author (with Andrew N. Scott) of *One Half the People: The Fight for Woman Suffrage* (University of Illinois Press, 1982).

Elizabeth Cady Stanton and Susan B.
Anthony, two of the early leaders in the
woman suffrage movement.

1: The Beginnings of Women's Rights in the U.S.

As of the mid nineteenth century, the right to vote and to participate in democratic decision making was still reserved exclusively to men. Women were considered by some people to be absorbed by the world of home and family, too emotional for politics, and insufficiently independent of mind and judgment. In 1848 a group of American reformers, women and men both, first advocated the political equality of the sexes and initiated the long drive toward woman suffrage.

The leading figure in this movement was Elizabeth Cady Stanton, a thirty-three-year-old mother of four sons, living in Seneca Falls, New York, a small manufacturing town on the Erie Canal. In 1848 she drafted a "Declaration of Sentiments" and presented it to a meeting of fellow protesters: "We hold these truths to be self-evident: that all men and women are created equal." This was the first manifesto of women's rights in American history. Like the Declaration of Independence, Stanton's woman's rights declaration included twelve resolutions. The most controversial was the ninth: "That it is the duty of the women of this country to secure to themselves the sacred right to the elective franchise."

In 1851 Stanton was introduced to Susan B. Anthony, a teacher five years her junior, who lived in nearby Rochester. They formed a political partnership which lasted fifty years. No individual embodies better than Anthony the spirit of determination of the woman suffrage movement; she remains an inspiring figure today.

The third great figure in the women's rights movement at this time was Lucy Stone. Stone, the first woman in the United States to receive a college degree (from Oberlin in Ohio), also made her mark by refusing to change her last name when she married Henry Blackwell in 1853. For many years, women who kept their own names upon marriage were called "Lucy Stoners." Lucy Stone is pictured here with her only child, Alice Stone Blackwell, who became an important twentieth-century suffragist.

Lucy Stone and daughter Alice Stone Blackwell in 1859. The long struggle for woman suffrage stretched over two generations. Both Stone and her daughter were important leaders in their times.

Proceedings of the Seneca Falls Convention, considered the first women's rights convention held in the United States. A second convention took place the next month in Rochester.

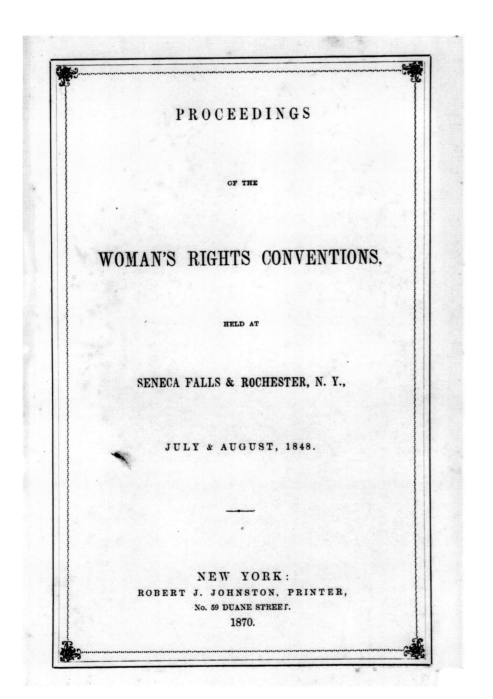

PROCEEDINGS

OF THE

WOMAN'S RIGHTS CONVENTIONS,

HELD AT

SENECA FALLS & ROCHESTER, N. Y.,

JULY & AUGUST, 1848.

NEW YORK:
ROBERT J. JOHNSTON, PRINTER,
No. 59 DUANE STREET.
1870.

The early supporters of the women's rights movement were drawn from other reform groups in which women were active. Anthony and Stone and, to a lesser degree, Stanton were all associated with abolitionism and spoke on the evils of slavery. The temperance movement was an equally important source for early women's rights supporters. Women were the victims of both the domestic violence and the drain on family finances caused by men's drinking. *The Lily,* a temperance newspaper published in Seneca Falls, included many articles on women's rights by Elizabeth Cady Stanton. *The Lily* also advocated a healthy alternative to the heavy skirts then worn by women; "the bloomer," a long and loose, divided skirt, was named after the paper's editor, Amelia Bloomer.

2: Moving into the Constitution: Woman Suffrage after the Civil War

During the Civil War, women suspended their drive for greater rights, but resumed it with renewed fervor after 1865. The right to vote was now their chief demand. Previously they had looked to the states to enfranchise them, but after the war they shifted their sights to the federal level. The U.S. Constitution was being dramatically amended: to abolish slavery (the Thirteenth Amendment), to establish national citizenship (the Fourteenth Amendment), and to bar disfranchisement by "race, color, or previous condition of servitude" (the Fifteenth Amendment). Women wanted the U.S. Constitution to guarantee their voting rights as well.

The American Equal Rights Association was formed in 1866 to link the causes of black and woman suffrage. But a year later, the passage of the Fourteenth Amendment, which limited the electorate to "male persons," dealt a serious blow to its platform of "universal suffrage." This precipitated some of the most divisive debates in the history of the drive for woman suffrage. At the 1867 meeting of the American Equal Rights Association, veteran African-American abolitionist George Downing accused woman suffragists of being "opposed to the enfranchisement of the colored man, unless the ballot should also be accorded to woman at the same time."

courtesy of Nell Painter

Sojourner Truth (née Isabella Van Wagener, 1797-1883). Carte-de-visite photograph, c. 1860. Truth, a great preacher and ex-slave, was a proponent of universal suffrage, male and female, black and white.

Rochester Nov. 5th 1872 —

Dear Mrs Stanton

Well I have been &
gone & done it!! — positively
voted the Republican ticket —
strait — this A.M. at 7 O'clock
& swore my vote in at that
— was registered on Friday & 15
other women followed suit
in this ward — then in Sundry
others some, 20 a thirty other
women tried to register, but
all save two were refused — all
our three sisters voted — Rhoda

Elizabeth Stanton responded that, if forced to make a choice, she would "demand that not another man be enfranchised without the woman by his side."

Caught between the divisive claims on behalf of white women and black men were women of color. At the same meetings at which Stanton and Downing clashed, the great orator Sojourner Truth weighed in on the side of universal suffrage. "There is a great stir about colored men getting their rights, but not a word about the colored women," she explained to the audience. ". . . I am for keeping the thing going while things are stirring; because if we wait till it is still, it will take a great while to get it going again." Born under slavery in 1797 as Isabella Van Wagener, this extraordinary woman changed her name to Sojourner Truth under the influence of religious revelation. She died in 1883.

In 1869 two rival suffrage organizations were formed—the National Woman Suffrage Association and the American Woman Suffrage Association. They differed over whether to support black suffrage without woman suffrage. By 1870 both the Fourteenth and Fifteenth Amendments had been ratified without including votes for women. But woman suffragists were not yet ready to give up. They now argued that the U.S. Constitution, properly understood, already allowed women to vote. Their argument was that women were national citizens, and that the supreme right of citizenship was the franchise. Based on this interpretation, hundreds of women around the country attempted to register and vote in 1872. Some convinced election officials to accept their ballots. Susan B. Anthony was one of these successful voters.

Three weeks after voting, Anthony was arrested by U.S. marshals for illegal voting. Despite her extraordinary efforts in arguing her case, a federal judge directed the jury to find her guilty. Fearful that she would appeal, the judge refused to jail her and only charged her a small fine, which she nonetheless refused to pay. In 1875 the United States Supreme Court ruled against the same claims in another "women's voting" case, *Minor* v. *Happersett*. Although willing to grant that women were U.S. citizens, the Court ruled that voting was not a right of national citizenship. This ruling against woman suffrage was part of the Court's larger retreat from the egalitarian spirit of Reconstruction.

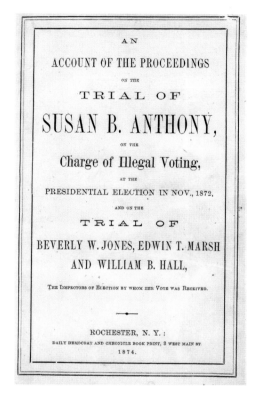

AN
ACCOUNT OF THE PROCEEDINGS
ON THE
TRIAL OF
SUSAN B. ANTHONY,
ON THE
Charge of Illegal Voting,
AT THE
PRESIDENTIAL ELECTION IN NOV., 1872,
AND ON THE
TRIAL OF
BEVERLY W. JONES, EDWIN T. MARSH
AND WILLIAM B. HALL,
THE INSPECTORS OF ELECTION BY WHOM HER VOTE WAS RECEIVED.

ROCHESTER, N. Y.:
DAILY DEMOCRAT AND CHRONICLE BOOK PRINT, 8 WEST MAIN ST
1874.

Since woman suffragists' efforts for federal enfranchisement had been thwarted, they directed their hopes back to the states. But a woman suffrage amendment to the United States Constitution remained their ultimate goal.

Oregon State Convention on Woman Suffrage held in Portland, Oregon, in 1905. Susan B. Anthony, age seventy-five years old, can be found in the center of the front row.

3: The Suffrage Movement Expands Westward, 1876-1896

In the late nineteenth century, the woman suffrage movement flourished in the West. Under frontier settlement conditions, traditional "eastern" notions of women's incapacity gave way to a rough and ready equality between the sexes. But there were other factors contributing to the West's greater openness to woman suffrage. White women's mission was supposedly to civilize the people and cultures displaced by America's westward expansion, and they claimed political power to aid them in this task. In addition, the rise of the Populist Party radicalized western politics in the 1890s, which greatly helped woman suffrage advocates.

In 1869 the Wyoming Legislature, in the hope of attracting more female settlers, made history by enfranchising the women of the Territory. A local woman, Esther Morris, is credited with educating the legislators about women's rights. In 1870 the women of Utah Territory were also enfranchised. The motivation of Utah legislators was to strengthen the political power of Mormons and to show the world how highly regarded women were in their society. But in 1887 the U.S. Congress moved to outlaw polygamy and deny the franchise to all women and to male polygamists in Utah. The women protested their impending

Frances Willard (1839-1898), president of the Woman's Christian Temperance Union, who encouraged members of the WCTU to support the suffrage cause.

Elizabeth Boynton Harbert –
Pres. of the E S Association of Ill., and your coworkers –

To you as you meet in your annual executive session we the women of Wyoming send – – –

Greeting.

We the women of Wyoming, conscious that we alone are the favored ones of earth, aim to do what we can to express our hearty cooperation in all movements, toward the securing of the ballot for woman, we who have been placed upon the very summit of freedom and the broad plain of universal equality gladly recognize in each of these movements an advance in the line of thought and in the securing of a right dear to the hearts of us all and a privilege we hasten to enjoy at all seasons – May the meeting

disfranchisement to show the larger world that, anti-Mormon prejudice notwithstanding, they were moral, self-regarding Christian women. Congress ignored their objections, but when Utah became a state in 1896, its legislators restored the right of Utah women to vote.

The Woman's Christian Temperance Union (WCTU), formed in 1874, was especially important among western women. In 1880 the WCTU's second president, Frances Willard, convinced its members to support woman suffrage, arguing that women needed the vote to destroy the liquor industry. Under Willard's "do everything policy," the WCTU became a highly political organization, with links to Populists and organized labor, but always committed to spreading family-centered values and Christian civilization. "Home Protection" was the WCTU's slogan for woman suffrage.

Another source of western suffrage support was agrarian radicalism. Members of the Grange, the Greenbacker Party, and the Populists were all inclined to support woman suffrage. Writing to Elizabeth Boynton Harbert, editor of a Chicago suffrage newspaper, a Missouri farm wife, Mrs. E. C. Chamberlain, insisted that "the idle rich" were not the only women who wanted to vote, but that hard-working farm wives like herself had strong political opinions that they wanted to make known. These women believed that federal currency policies unfairly favored eastern bankers and railroad magnates; but they also objected that "the ignorant negro or foreigner" had political rights which they, as white American women, were denied. This combination of antagonism toward the rich and resentment of "the negro and the foreigner" has always helped to fuel the powerful tradition of American populism.

In 1890 agrarian protests culminated in the formation of the Populist Party. With its support, suffragists were able to get state legislatures to authorize a series of voter referenda on woman suffrage. The first of these elections, in 1893 in Colorado, was successful, making Colorado the first state (as opposed to territory) to enfranchise women by action of a majority of male voters. However, of the five other referenda that took place during the Populist insurgency of the 1890s, only one in Idaho passed. As of 1896, four states, all of them west of the Mississippi, permitted women full voting rights.

FRANK LESLIE'S ILLUSTRATED NEWSPAPER

Entered according to Act of Congress, in the year 1888, by Mrs. Frank Leslie, in the Office of the Librarian of Congress at Washington.—Entered at the Post Office, New York, N. Y., as Second-class Matter.

No. 1,732.—Vol. LXVII.]   NEW YORK—FOR THE WEEK ENDING NOVEMBER 24, 1888.   [PRICE, 10 CENTS.

WOMAN SUFFRAGE IN WYOMING TERRITORY.—SCENE AT THE POLLS IN CHEYENNE.
FROM A PHOTO. BY KIRKLAND.—SEE PAGE 733.

4: Coming to California, 1871-1910

Ellen Clark Sargent led the California woman suffrage movement in the 1890s. The California Woman Suffrage Association was run from her home.

Susan B. Anthony and Rev. Dr. Anna Shaw being entertained by the San Diego Club, June 20, 1895.

The California campaign of 1896 was one of the last and most important referenda of the populist era. The size of the state and its potential for growth made it a very important prize for suffragists to win.

Ellen Clark Sargent was representative of the powerful, wealthy women who led the California woman suffrage movement in the 1890s. Sargent was the widow of Aaron A. Sargent, the U.S. Senator from California, who had first proposed a federal woman suffrage amendment to the U.S. Constitution in 1878. Because Sargent was a lawyer associated with the Southern Pacific Railroad, Mrs. Sargent was able to provide free railroad transportation throughout the state to suffrage organizers. She was a profound admirer of Susan B. Anthony and lavished personal attention on her during Anthony's several trips to California in connection with the 1896 campaign. Anthony traveled in the company of Anna Howard Shaw, her protégée and later president of the National American Woman Suffrage Association. Jane Stanford, co-founder of Stanford University, was also a major backer of woman suffrage in California and a close friend of Anthony's. Seventy-five years old, Anthony spent eight months in California and traveled from San Francisco

Letter from Lulu Pile Little to women's club leader Caroline Severance, November 6, 1896. The defeat of the first California referendum on woman suffrage was largely due to the San Francisco area. In this letter Little suggests splitting the state in half.

as far as Los Angeles and San Diego to build support for woman suffrage.

Support from state Republicans and Populists seemed to promise victory in California in 1896, but just before the election, the Democratic and Populist parties fused around the issue of "free silver," and woman suffrage became expendable. Deserted by all major parties, woman suffrage still won an impressive forty-five percent of the popular vote. Woman suffrage carried Los Angeles County, but the margin of defeat came from San Francisco and Alameda counties, where labor opposition and anti-Asian sentiments doomed votes for women. The defeat of woman suffrage was a crushing blow to the movement in the state, and recovery took almost a decade.

In 1906 the woman suffrage movement in California suffered two more blows: the death of Susan B. Anthony and the catastrophic San Francisco earthquake and fire. One of the consequences of the earthquake was to shift California reform energies, including those of woman suffragists, south to Los Angeles. Four years later, Los Angeles suffragists convinced the legislature to authorize another woman suffrage referendum and give California voters a second chance to enfranchise the women of their state.

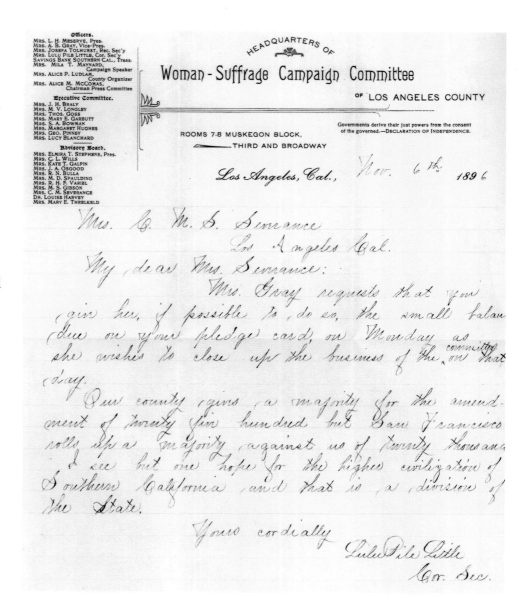

Suffragists march to Republican party convention in Oakland, California, 1908. This was reportedly the only such parade that took place in California.

5: The 1911 California Campaign Begins: Assembling a Winning Coalition

In 1910 Progressives took over the Republican Party and elected Hiram Johnson as governor in California. In the wake of this dramatic change in state politics, woman suffrage advocates were able to convince state legislators to include votes for women as part of a special election scheduled nine months later, in October 1911.

Middle-class club women, the source of most volunteer workers for civic reforms in this period, played an important role in the brief period suffragists had to reach the voters of California. Club women argued the importance of woman suffrage as a weapon against widespread municipal corruption. "Women are, by nature and training, housekeepers," they said. "Let them have a hand in the city's housekeeping, even if they introduce an occasional house-cleaning."

The leading figure in the Los Angeles women's club movement was Caroline Severance, founder of the city's most influential civic organization, the Friday Morning Club. Born in 1820, the same year as Susan B. Anthony, she lived long enough to become a voter and was believed to be the first woman in Los Angeles to register, once the referendum had passed. Katherine Edson, also a club woman, led the

WOMEN IN THE HOME

We are forever being told that the place for women is in the HOME. Well, so be it. But what do we expect of her in the home? Merely to stay in the home is not enough. She is a failure unless she attends to the health and welfare, moral as well as physical, of her family, and especially of her children. She, more than anyone else, is held responsible for what they become.

SHE is responsible for the cleanliness of her house.
SHE is responsible for the wholesomeness of the food.
SHE is responsible for the children's health.
She, above all, is responsible for their morals.

HOW FAR CAN THE MOTHER CONTROL THESE THINGS?

She can **clean her own rooms, BUT** if the neighbors are allowed to live in filth, she cannot keep her rooms from being filled with bad air and smells, or from being infested with vermin.

She can **cook her food well, BUT** if dealers are permitted to sell poor food, unclean milk or stale eggs, she cannot make the food wholesome for her children.

She can **care for her own plumbing and refuse, BUT** if the plumbing in the rest of the house is unsanitary, if garbage accumulates and the halls and stairs are left dirty, she cannot protect her children from the sickness and infection resulting.

She can **take every care to avoid fire, BUT** if the house has been badly built, if the fire-escapes are inadequate, she cannot guard her children from the horrors of being maimed or killed by fire.

She can **open her windows** to give her children the air that we are told is so necessary, **BUT** if the air is laden with infection, with tuberculosis and other contagious diseases, she cannot protect her children from this danger.

She can **send her children out** for air and exercise, **BUT** if the conditions that surround them on the streets are immoral and degrading, she cannot protect them from these dangers.

Alone, she cannot make these things right. Who or what can?

The city can do it—the **city government** that is **elected by the people,** to take care of the interests **of the people.**

And **who decides** what the city government shall do?

FIRST, the officials of that government; and, **SECOND,** those who elect them.

Do the women elect them? **NO,** the men do. So it is the **Men** and **not** the women who are really **responsible** for the

Unclean Houses	Bad Plumbing
Unwholesome Food	Danger of Fire
Risk of Tuberculosis and Other Diseases	
Immoral Influences of the Street	

In fact, **MEN** are responsible for the conditions under which the children live, but we hold **WOMEN** responsible for the results of those conditions. If we hold women responsible for the results, must we not, in simple justice, let them **have something to say** as to what these conditions shall be? There is one simple way of doing this. Give them the same means that men have. **LET THEM VOTE.**

Women are, by nature and training, housekeepers. Let them have a hand in the city's housekeeping, even if they introduce an occasional house-cleaning.

[Courtesy of the National American Woman Suffrage Association.]

This leaflet, entitled Women in the Home, *suggests that with the vote, women will use their natural housekeeping skills to rid the city of municipal corruption.*

Suffrage leaflets in German, French, and Italian. In order to reach all corners of California's diverse population, suffrage organizations published leaflets in a variety of languages.

Frauen Haben Eine Allgemeine Wahlstimme

—IN—

| Australien | Norwegen | Insel Man |
| New Seeland | Finnland | Tasmania |

Frauen Haben Die Municipale Wahl

—IN—

England	Island	Dännemark
Schottland	Canada	Schweden
Wales	Natal (Süd Africa)	

IN DEN VEREINIGTEN STAATEN

WÄHLEN FRAUEN

IN ACHT UND ZWANZIG STAATEN

In Municipalen und Schul Angelegenheiten

Frauen Wählen Unter Gleichen Bedingungen
Wie Die Manner In

Wyoming
Utah
Colorado
Idaho
Washington

Varum Nicht In California ?

LISEZ — RÉFLÉCHISSEZ

Les Femmes ont le droit de
Voter
à toutes les élections

—en—

| Australie | Norvège | Ile de Man |
| Nouvelle Zélande | Finlande | Tasmanie |

Elles votent aux élections municipales

—en—

Angleterre	Islande .	Danemark
Ecosse	Canada	Suède
Pays de Galles	Natal (Afrique)	

AUX ETATS UNIS

Les femmes votent aux élections municipales et scolaires dans

28 ETATS

Elles ont le même droit de voter que les hommes dans les états suivants:

Wyoming	depuis	1870
Colorado	depuis	1893
Idaho	depuis	1896
Utah	depuis	1896
Washington	depuis	1910

ET EN CALIFORNIE ??

En France, un project de loi a été déposé, il y a deux ans environ, à la Chambre tendant à donner à la femme le droit de voter, comme à l'homme. Nous laisserons nous dépasser ici?

Le Donne Hanno Completo Suffragio

—IN—

| Australia | Norvegia | Isle of Man |
| Nuova Zelanda | Filanda | Tasmania |

Le Donne Hanno Suffragio Municipale

—IN—

Inghilterra	Iceland	Danimarca
Scozia	Canada	Sweden
Wales	Natal (Sud Africa)	

NEGLI STATI UNITI

LE DONNE VOTANO

IN VENTOTTO STATI

In Affari Municipali E Scolastici

Le Donne Hanno Ugual Suffragio Degli
Uomini Negli Stati

Wyoming
Utah
Colorado
Idaho
Washington

Perché Non In California ?

---

suffrage lobby in the state legislature through the winter of 1910-1911. After her success with the suffrage referendum bill, she was appointed by Governor Johnson to the California Division of Industrial Welfare. It was asserted that because of her efforts by the 1920s California had achieved a higher average wage for women than any other state in the Union.

Wage-earning women, who were coming together in labor unions and demanding political power, became another important element in the woman suffrage coalition. Frances Nacke Noel, a German-born labor activist and socialist, was the leading working-class suffragist in Los Angeles. With the help of the Los Angeles Central Labor Council, she organized the Wage Earners Suffrage League among working women. In Northern California, Maud Younger was the most important link between organized labor and the woman suffrage movement. Although born to a wealthy California family, she dedicated herself to the labor movement. Known as "the millionaire waitress" for her role in unionizing the waitresses and barmaids of San Francisco, she is credited with doing much of the work to win the support of the powerful San Francisco labor movement for the cause. Many observers thought that increased support from the San Francisco labor unions may well have made the winning difference in 1911.

Though virtually unrepresented in the leadership of the suffrage movement, immigrants were a crucial part of the electorate, and without their support votes for women could never have hoped to win. California suffragists published and distributed a large quantity of campaign literature in "foreign languages" and brought the suffrage message to churches, clubs, and other organizations where immigrant communities gathered.

6: Advertising Votes for Women

Because suffrage activists could not rely on regular political party machinery for support, they experimented with new ways to get out the vote, giving their campaign a distinctly modern flair. They drew especially on the techniques of commercial advertising. "Although the proposition that women should vote is seriously and profoundly true," explained a state leader, "it will at first be established . . . much as the virtues of a breakfast food are established, by affirmation." The advertising dynamic went both ways. As the number of women consumers who were strongly identified with votes for women grew, commercial enterprises sought to identify their products with the cause. One such product was named "The Suffragette Cracker;" the term "suffragette" was initially a derisive term used by the British press, but it was later embraced as a term of pride by suffrage activists in the United States.

Advertisement for Shredded Wheat used the issue of woman suffrage to sell its products.

Materials used to spread the suffrage message included postcards, calendars, playing cards, ink blotters, flower seed packets, and The Woman Suffrage Cook Book.

Alice Park, a Palo Alto journalist, was a major advocate of modern advertising methods. Suffrage leaflets, she argued, needed to be enlivened by bright color, large type, and easy-to-read imagery. Color was especially important in suffrage iconography. "We made good use of color in our California campaign," wrote Park. "We knew the suffragettes in England tried to catch the eye with colors and our yellow was easier to use than their purple, white, and green. . . . We said it was the most beautiful color in the world, and especially in the golden state; that California owed its life to the gold in the hills; that the golden poppy is the state flower; that the golden orange grows here, and golden grain."

In California, Park popularized what she called "personal advertising," everything from lapel buttons to suffrage stationary to baggage stickers. Such clever, light-hearted novelties implicitly challenged the assumption that suffragists were old fashioned, humorless, and stern. Inasmuch as shopping was considered an appropri-

ate activity for women, these mass-produced commodities may also have been less disturbing to male voters than more conventional political techniques. Because of the success of the California campaign, subsequent suffrage campaigns were much more inventive and eye catching in their propaganda work. Was there a down side to the relentless "advertising" of woman suffrage? Perhaps woman suffrage itself came to be seen as a novelty, for the great campaigns to win the vote for women were soon forgotten after 1920.

The special election of October 10, 1911, was called to consider a series of progressive political reforms designed to increase the power of the people over politicians and powerful economic interests. Along with votes for women, the ballot included proposals for the initiative and recall, railroad regulation, workmen's compensation, and charter governments for counties.

Fraudulent voting was a real concern in early twentieth-century elections. Automatic voting machines had not yet been developed, and voters had to mark their ballots by hand. The woman suffrage measure was the fourth item, and suffragists felt that this gave them some protection against illiterate voters who might have been instructed to vote against the measure as identified by its place on the ballot.

Given the expectation of a close vote on October 10, every vote in favor of woman suffrage was crucial. J. L. Edmunds, publisher of *The Liberator*, a local African-American newspaper, argued that Los Angeles' five thousand African-American voters could make a difference in the outcome of the referendum. However, Caroline Severance, the venerable white reformer to whom Edmunds wrote, opposed the integration of African-American women into

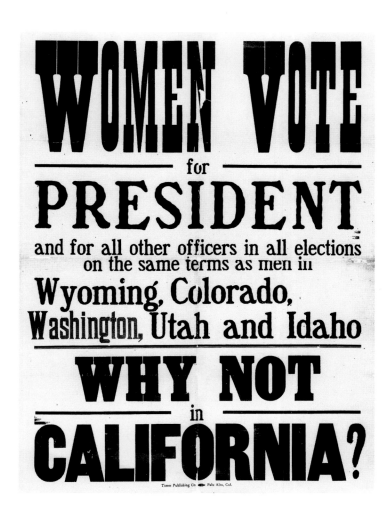

This pro-suffrage poster from the California campaign lists the states where women have the right to vote, and asks, "Why not in California?"

One of the first Chinese-American women to vote in California.

the Los Angeles woman suffrage effort. Despite the hostility of white suffragists to interracial cooperation, other groups of African Americans were also involved in the 1911 referendum. In Oakland, for instance, the Colored Women's Suffrage League worked to get out the vote.

The day before the election, anti-suffragists placed a full page advertisement in the *San Francisco Chronicle*. The advertisement cost $500, which may have come from the liquor industry and other economic interests fearful of women's reforming zeal. The "antis" argued that by moving into the male political sphere, women would lose their lofty moral influence. Underlying such rhetoric was a much deeper anxiety about the connection between votes for women, women's growing economic independence, and changes in traditional family life. Suffrage opponents were, in essence, protesting the broader and more radical feminism that they suspected underlay the specific demand for the vote.

On October 10, 1911, suffragists were at the polling places to make sure the vote count was accurate. As the tallies began to come in, the referendum appeared to be going down to defeat. However, when all the numbers were totaled, woman suffrage had won by a

tiny margin of less than 4000 votes. Alice Park wrote that she believed that "the San Francisco vote was changed [by referendum opponents] to make sure of defeat," but that the antis had underestimated the strength of the pro-suffrage forces and had not given themselves a large enough margin to defeat the referendum. California became the sixth "star in the suffrage flag," the first large industrial state to enfranchise women.

After their October victory, women were eager to register, especially in Los Angeles, where a hotly contested election for mayor, pitting a Progressive Republican against a Socialist, was scheduled for November. Over 80,000 Los Angeles women registered in the first weeks. They may have provided the margin of victory for the Republican candidate, George Alexander over Socialist Job Harriman.

Although the woman suffrage referendum removed the language restricting the electorate to men, federal prohibitions against the naturalization of Asian immigrants remained intact. Nonetheless, a handful of Chinese-American women, who were citizens because they had been born in the United States, successfully registered and voted with other members of their sex.

Anti-suffrage advertisement, To the Voters of Northern California, *which appeared in the* San Francisco Chronicle *on the eve of the California election in October 1911.*

TO THE VOTERS OF NORTHERN CALIFORNIA

We, the women of the Northern California Association Opposed to Woman Suffrage, urge you not to thrust the womanhood of this State into the political arena, at the request of the small minority of women who are asking for the ballot.

Mrs. Harriet Stanton Blatch, one of the leaders of the world suffrage movement, in Pearson's Magazine, February, 1910, said:

"I've given up the American woman. She's hopeless. If it depends upon her, women will never have the ballot!"

The National Woman Suffrage Organization circulated an appeal in this State during this campaign in which, under the signature of Jessie Ashley, national treasurer, it is admitted that there are only 75,000 organized Suffragists in the United States, working among 93,000,000 people, and that the 75,000 organized Suffragettes are not sufficiently interested in the agitation to give a dollar each to the movement.

In 1895 the question of woman suffrage was put to a referendum vote of the women of Massachusetts. Out of nearly half a million women who might have voted on the question only 22,000 were sufficiently interested to cast a vote either way.

Since that time the Suffragists have fought every attempt to put the question to a vote of the women, even as they fought it here in California.

When in the polling booth, we ask you to remember that the vast majority of California women do not want to vote.

We ask you not to put upon our shoulders the responsibility of man's work.

The advance of woman—moral, intellectual and economic—has been made without the vote.

Woman now stands outside of politics and may appeal to any party on matters of education and reform.

The ballot does not govern the law of supply and demand, and so cannot affect the wages of woman. It has never raised the wages of man—why should it be expected to do so for woman?

The woman suffrage movement is a backward step in the progress of civilization. Do not permit California to take a step backward.

Women Are Not Free in Suffrage States.

In his story, "The Beast," on page 307, Judge Ben Lindsey has this to say of the Hon. Alma Lafferty: "I went at the beginning of the campaign to practically all the woman's suffrage leaders, who, at national meetings, had been telling how much the women had done for the Juvenile Court in Denver;

and none of them dared help 'ac. Women like Mrs. Mary C. Bradford and Mrs. Lafferty (who was a member of the last Legislature) took the platform against me and supported the System in its attempt to 'get' the Juvenile Court."

On page 306 of the same volume, Judge Lindsey says: "I talked to a number of school teachers . . . they told me they dared not make themselves conspicuous . . . the teachers were afraid of losing their positions."

On page 307 of "The Beast," Judge Lindsey says again: "If anyone believes that woman suffrage is a panacea for all the evils of political life, he does not know what those evils are . . . The women are as helpless as the rest of us . . . They are bound by the same bread-and-butter consideration as the rest of us. Their leaders in politics are politicians; when they get their nominations, from the corporate machines, they do the work of the corporations, and there is almost no way . . . to get a party nomination except from a corporation machine. Women in politics are human beings; they are not 'ministering angels' of an ethereal ideality; and they are unable to free us, because they are not free themselves."

Suffrage Leaders Abuse Their Freedom.

Rev. Anna Shaw, President of the National Woman's Suffrage Association, says:

"I would make motherhood a Governmental institution. I would pension all mothers and have them provided for, first to last, by the State. I believe that motherhood should be independent of man.

"One crying need of our civilization is the presence of women on the police force. I would place a woman policeman at the door of every saloon and dance hall, every nickel theater and every factory."

Mrs. Carrie Chapman Catt, President of the International Woman Suffrage Alliance, says:

"I believe that the time will come, and that comparatively soon, when every American woman who does not earn her own living will be considered a prostitute."

These are the lengths to which the leaders of this movement are willing to go, and any one who favors it, favors them, and must be ready to take the consequence.

Is This a Direct Blow at the American Home?

Mrs. Harriet Stanton Blatch, one of the leaders of the world suffrage movement, said in her discussion of the economic emancipation of woman that she rejoiced in every co-operative working woman's dwelling, because it aimed a blow at the isolated house, and she repeated her proposition regarding the institutional care of children.

Another leading Suffragist, in an article on woman's work in America, says: "Suffrage aims to benefit woman by recognizing her as a perfect equal of man, politically and socially, and by fixing woman's means of support by the State so as to render her independent of man."

Nothing Sacred to Suffragists.

The Suffragists have travestied the Bible, the Declaration of Independence and the American flag.

They have travestied the Bible with their "Woman's Bible," in which they take exception to the Creator as a Heavenly Father, instead of a Divine Pair.

They have travestied the Declaration of Independence—have mocked the most hallowed document of the Nation, and assert that man "has made her (woman), if married, in the eye of the law, civilly dead. He has endeavored, in every way that he could, to destroy her confidence in her own powers, to lessen her self-respect and to make her willing to lead a dependent and abject life."

The tenth count in the Suffrage Declaration of Independence is: "He has usurped the prerogative of Jehovah himself, claiming it is his right to assign for her a sphere of action, when that belongs to her consciousness and her God."

The editors add: "Quite as many false ideas prevail as to woman's true position in the home as elsewhere. Womanhood is the great fact of her life, motherhood and wifehood are but incidental relations."

The American Flag is not good enough for the Suffragists. They have made a mockery of the National emblem, by flaunting the flag with but five stars in the field, signifying that only those five States in which women vote are worthy a representation on the National emblem.

WOMEN DON'T WANT BALLOT.

The great majority of California women do not follow the suffrage flag; they do not want to vote; they depend upon the manhood of California to protect them from the responsibility of the ballot. They rely on manhood suffrage and a safe and sane government.

Vote Against the Woman Suffrage Amendment!

ISSUED BY

The Women of Northern California Association Opposed to Woman Suffrage

Suffrage march in New York in 1913. The women are carrying portable rostrums from which they spoke to the crowds.

8: Moving up to the National Stage: Organizing Women's Votes

State-by-state victories could only take woman suffrage so far. In 1915 Massachusetts, New Jersey, Pennsylvania, and New York voted on woman suffrage. In New York, then the most populous state in the Union, the campaign cost well over $100,000. Faced with much stiffer opposition than in California, however, all of the 1915 campaigns went down to heartbreaking defeat. At this point, many suffragists began to shift their efforts from the state toward the national arena. The character of the American constitutional system has often provided activists with the strategic option of moving to the federal level when blocked in the states and vice versa.

In 1913 an upstart suffrage organization named the Congressional Union was formed. Its goal was to persuade the U. S. Congress to pass a woman suffrage amendment to the federal constitution. Even though it was focused on the national arena, the Congressional Union understood that successful state campaigns provided the suffrage movement with a crucial weapon: the votes of women themselves. While the majority of suffrag-

Sara Field, Ingeborg Kindstedt, and Maria Kindberg drove from San Francisco to Washington, D.C., in 1915, spreading the message that the voting women of the West would vote against Democratic Congressmen if the party did not support the woman suffrage amendment.

ists continued their slow educational campaigns, the radicals of the Congressional Union appealed to the women of the "suffrage states" to use their new voting power on behalf of woman suffrage. The Congressional Union attracted a younger, more modern generation of suffragists, who were impatient with the constraints placed on Victorian ladies.

Although they already had the vote, the women of California joined in the Congressional Union campaign for national suffrage. In 1915 Sara Bard Field, an Oregon-born poet, accompanied by Rhode Island sisters Ingeborg Kindstedt and Maria Kindberg, served as "envoys from the West" and carried a petition containing 500,000 signatures gathered at the Pan Pacific Exposition in San Francisco to Washington, D.C. Their message was that the voting women of the West would organize against the Democratic Party because it did not support a woman suffrage amendment to the U.S. Constitution. Traveling on unpaved and barely marked roads, they took almost a month to drive from California to Chicago.

In 1916 the Congressional Union renamed itself the Woman's Party. Another set of "suffrage envoys," this time from the East, came West to ask women voters to vote against President Woodrow Wilson because of his party's opposition to the amendment. Inez Milholland Boissevain, a thirty-year-old lawyer from New York, was the star speaker. At a large suffrage rally in Los Angeles, Boissevain collapsed from the rigors of the campaign, dramatically calling out for votes for women as she fell. A few weeks later she died from the complications of pneumonia. The Woman's Party declared her a martyr to the cause of woman suffrage.

As war clouds gathered over Europe, it became harder to organize women's votes against the Democratic Party for its stand against woman suffrage. The question of whether to promote votes for women as a single issue or as one of the many political matters on which women wanted the right to vote came up repeatedly. Despite the efforts of the Woman's Party, many women felt they had to support President Wilson, who was campaigning on a peace platform. In 1916 Wilson was reelected to a second term.

California suffragist Kitty Marion in her white suffrage "uniform."

Poster of Inez Milholland Boissevain, who became a martyr in the cause following her death on the woman suffrage campaign trail in Los Angeles in 1916.

INEZ MILHOLLAND BOISSEVAIN

INTO LIGHT

WHO DIED FOR THE FREEDOM OF WOMEN.

courtesy of Ellen DuBois

The Woman's Party journal, The Suffragist, *celebrates the Senate's passage of
the woman suffrage amendment to the
U.S. Constitution.*

9: The War, Civil Disobedience, and the Nineteenth Amendment

Alice Paul was the founder and driving spirit behind the Woman's Party. A Philadelphia Quaker and a veteran of the dramatic British suffragette campaign, Paul combined non-violence and militance in her leadership style. She led the Woman's Party's shift from an electoral strategy to one of civil disobedience. Years before, British suffragettes had gained international headlines when they were arrested and force fed for protesting parliamentary inaction. In January 1917, American activists began to picket the White House peacefully. Four months later, Congress voted to take the country into war. (The first woman elected to Congress, Jeanette Rankin of Montana, voted against the war resolution.) At this point, peaceful picketing became treason. Suffragists carried signs questioning whether the United States could truly lead a crusade for democracy if its own women were disfranchised; for this they were assaulted by crowds and arrested by police. Ultimately almost three hundred women, representing a truly extraordinary range of individuals, from munitions workers to wives of Congressmen, were arrested for civil disobedience.

As the number of arrests and length of sentences increased, jailed suffragists fought back with hunger strikes and

Alice Paul, founder of the Woman's Party which brought increased militancy to the suffrage movement.

Once the U.S. entered the war, the practice of picketing the White House was met with arrests, jailing, and force-feeding. The resulting public outrage helped lead to the passage of the suffrage amendment.

demands that they be treated as political prisoners. Prison officials responded with painful "forced feeding," using a tube running through the nose into the stomach. In November 1917, Alice Paul herself was arrested and placed in the prison's psychopathic ward. However, the arrests actually increased public pressure to solve the suffrage issue. By January 1918, the House of Representatives gave the woman suffrage amendment the two-thirds vote it needed to pass.

Only after the war ended did President Wilson come out in favor of woman suffrage. He hoped that women voters would give him support for his vision of a League of Nations. Even with Wilson's prodding, however, the Senate was extremely slow to act on the amendment. Senate opposition to woman suffrage came especially from southern Democrats, who feared the enfranchisement of any more African Americans. Neither the radicals of the Woman's Party nor the more conventional suffragists of the National American Woman Suffrage Association challenged the racism of the southern Democrats. Instead, they argued that the enfranchisement of white women would guarantee white supremacy in the South. Even so, many African-American women were

suffrage activists. After the ratification of the Nineteenth Amendment, large numbers attempted to use their new votes, only to run up against the same *de facto* disfranchisement used against black men.

The Senate finally acted eighteen months after the House in June 1919. The final obstacle in the difficult process of passing a constitutional amendment was ratification by thirty-six of the nation's forty-eight state legislatures. This took another fifteen months. California was the eighteenth state to ratify. When the Tennessee legislature ratified the amendment by one vote in August 1920, woman suffrage became the law of the land. It had been seventy-two years since the Seneca Falls Convention in 1848.

After the Nineteenth Amendment was finally ratified in 1920, Alice Paul began to pursue another constitutional amendment to ensure full equality for women before the law. This became known as the Equal Rights Amendment (ERA). Paul led the fight for this amendment from 1923 until her death in 1971. In 1972, the U.S. Congress passed the Equal Rights Amendment, but it was never fully ratified.

10: Woman Suffrage as an International Movement

Frustrated for so long in their efforts to become voting citizens of their own countries, woman suffragists came to see themselves as sister citizens of the world. In the late nineteenth and early twentieth centuries, international women's organizations were established, allowing women from different nations to form lasting bonds with each other. These organizations, with their national affiliates, continue to exist today as the International Council of Women, the Women's International League for Peace and Freedom, and the International Alliance of Women. To this can be added the United Nations Conference on Women, which in 1995 conducted its fourth convocation of women activists from around the world.

The first of these organizations, the International Council of Women, had its beginnings in 1883, when Elizabeth Cady Stanton and Susan B. Anthony saw the potential for regular contact among women of different nations. Five years later, to commemorate the fortieth anniversary of Seneca Falls, American suffragists sponsored a grand meeting in Washington, D.C., attended by women of ten different nations, at which the International Council of Women was established.

Woman suffrage banner from Hungary, 1913, which reads, "Voting Rights for Women."

WOMAN SUFFRAGE
CALENDAR

1936

This organization was not limited to suffragists, but included women with many different reform goals, such as temperance and the cessation of international prostitution. In 1906 a second international organization, the International Woman Suffrage Alliance, was founded to concentrate on votes for women. Later it became the International Alliance of Women.

Woman suffrage movements have continued to grow around the world. Since 1920, the focus has shifted to Latin America, Asia, and Africa. The movement for woman suffrage has been particularly energetic and sustained in the Philippines. As early as 1909, middle-class Filipino women requested the vote on equal terms with men. When the islands became a Commonwealth in 1934, women's demands for the vote were put off by the government's requirement that a special plebiscite be held among the women themselves two years later. Women from all classes organized and registered for this election, and they voted overwhelmingly in favor of their permanent enfranchisement. In 1986, with the election of Corazon Aquino, the Philippines joined the growing club of nations with a woman as head of state.

Delegates to the 1913 International
Congress of Women meeting held in
Budapest.

913 Budapest. Internat. Cong. Women.

This selection of buttons and badges are part of a larger collection of such items assembled by Alice Park. Among those shown are button for the International Council of Women, a photographic button of Susan B. Anthony, and the special badge worn by Anna Howard Shaw at the last suffrage convention she attended before her death in 1919.

II: Preserving the History of the Woman Suffrage Movement

Many, perhaps most, past events have not outlived the memories of the people who experienced them. The reason we know so much about the woman suffrage movement is that participants deliberately preserved the history of the movement for posterity. They were proud of themselves for doing things that women had never done before. In addition, they wanted future generations to know how and why the status of women had changed and who was responsible.

The preserved record of woman suffrage begins with the multi-volumed *History of Woman Suffrage.* Susan B. Anthony conceived the idea of the *History* in 1876. She edited the first three volumes (along with Elizabeth Stanton, Matilda Joslyn Gage, and Ida Husted Harper), acted as publisher, and distributed copies at her own expense to individuals and libraries throughout the United States and abroad. No other reform campaign in American history took as much care to document itself as the woman suffrage movement.

In 1899 Susan B. Anthony offered her private library of women's rights books and pamphlets to the Library of Congress, which eagerly accepted it. At the

Letter to Susan B. Anthony from Ainsworth Spofford on behalf of the Library of Congress, acknowledging the donation of her papers.

Articles of agreement made and entered into this fifteenth day of November, 1876, by and between Elizabeth Cady Stanton of New Jersey, Matilda Joslyn Gage and Susan B. Anthony of the State of New York.

For and in consideration of one dollar and the mutual agreement hereinafter made, the said parties hereby enter into a partnership for the purpose of preparing and editing a history of the woman suffrage movement, — under the general name and title of A History of Woman Suffrage — securing its publication, and a sale for the same, and they do hereby agree to, and with each other that the said Elizabeth Cady Stanton, and the said Matilda Joslyn Gage shall write collect, select and arrange the material for said history; and the said Susan B. Anthony, shall, as her part of the work, and as an equivalent for the work done by said Elizabeth Cady Stanton, and said Matilda Joslyn Gage, secure the publication of said work by and through some competent publishing house; and the said Elizabeth Cady Stanton Matilda Joslyn Gage and Susan B. Anthony

"Articles of agreement made and entered into this fifteenth day of November, 1876, by and between Elizabeth Cady Stanton of New Jersey, Matilda Joslyn Gage and Susan B. Anthony of the State of New York.

For and in consideration of one dollar and the mutual agreement hereinafter made, the said parties hereby enter into a partnership for the purpose of preparing and editing a history of the woman suffrage movement,—under the general name and title of <u>A History of Woman Suffrage</u>—securing its publication, and a sale for the same, and they do hereby agree to, and with each other that the said Elizabeth Cady Stanton, and the said Matilda Joslyn Gage shall write, collect, select and arrange the material for said history; and the said Susan B. Anthony shall, as her part of the work, and as an equivalent for the work done by said Elizabeth Cady Stanton, and said Matilda Joslyn Gage, secure the publication of said work by and through some competent publishing house; and the said Elizabeth Cady Stanton, Matilda Joslyn Gage and Susan B. Anthony agree that the net profits of the history if there shall be any, shall be equally divided between the said parties, share and share alike.

They also agree that if one of the parties herein named, shall advance money toward the publication of said history, the profits of the work, if any, shall first go to the re-payment of that money advanced towards the publication of said history, and after the liquidation of said debt, the profits of the history, if any, shall be equally divided between said parties share and share alike. The said Elizabeth Cady Stanton, Matilda Joslyn Gage, and Susan B. Anthony agree that the book shall be entitled   . They also agree that the copyright shall be taken out in the names of all three of the parties, unless from the plan of its publication it shall be found necessary to have it taken out in the name of the publisher.

They furthermore agree that the three names of Elizabeth Cady Stanton, Matilda Joslyn Gage and Susan B. Anthony shall stand on the title-page of the above named history, as editors of the same.

They still further agree that the Publisher of the work shall make returns of sales to Susan B. Anthony, and that she shall render monthly accounts and make monthly payments to her associations, of the same.

It is furthermore agreed upon by the above named parties, that no promise, or payment of money for any purpose connected with this history, by either one of the above named parties shall be binding upon either of the others individually, or as editors of said history, without the consent of each and every one of them in writing, _previous_ to the promise, or payment of such money.

Said book shall be completed and published as soon as possible, without undue hindrance from either one of the above named parties.

By mutual agreement, and the relinquishment of these partnership papers, (of which each one shall have a duplicate copy) this partnership may come to an end, or now and different arrangements be entered into.

Signed, sealed and delivered in the presence of each other, and of these witnesses,

(signed) Elizabeth Cady Stanton
(signed) Matilda Joslyn Gage
(signed) Susan B. Anthony

witnesses: (signed) Margaret L. Stanton, Tenafly, New Jersey (signed) Fannie Simmons, Tenafly, New Jersey (signed) Scott Thompson, Tenafly, New Jersey"

Alice Park, California suffrage leader and unofficial historian of the movement, whose collections form the core of The Huntington's woman suffrage materials.

time, the Library of Congress intended to pay special attention to "the whole field of woman's history, condition, development, relation to institutions and intellectual and industrial activities." Over time, Anthony's books and pamphlets were absorbed into the general book collection, but can still be found today, with their owner's distinctive book plate, in the stacks of the Library of Congress.

The Huntington Library's rich and varied set of woman suffrage materials is largely due to a single individual, the veteran suffragist Alice Park of Palo Alto, California. After the passage of the Nineteenth Amendment in 1920, Park spent the next thirty years gathering suffrage and feminist materials from around the world. She was particularly proud of her collection of suffrage pins and badges, which at one time totaled more than 175 items. Many of these came from meetings she attended during her global travels in connection with the International Council of Women and the International Woman Suffrage Association. Park's collection is dedicated to Susan B. Anthony, who personified for her the suffrage movement. Originally deposited at the Los Angeles Public Library in 1941, the Susan B. Anthony Memorial Collection and other elements of Alice Park's collecting zeal have since made their way to the Huntington Library in San Marino, California.

Brief Chronology of the History of Woman Suffrage

1848   First women's rights convention, Seneca Falls, New York.

1851   Sojourner Truth asks, "Ain't I a Woman" at Women's Rights Convention.

1865   Thirteenth Amendment ratified, slavery constitutionally abolished.

1868   Fourteenth Amendment ratified, establishing national citizenship and introducing "that word male" into the U.S. Constitution.

1869   Two national suffrage societies founded, the National Woman Suffrage Association and the American Woman Suffrage Association. Wyoming Territory enacts woman suffrage.

1870   Utah Territory enacts woman suffrage.

1872   Susan B. Anthony and many other women cast their votes in presidential election; Anthony arrested for illegal voting.

1875   U.S. Supreme Court decision in *Minor* v. *Happersett* against women's claims to have the right to vote as national citizens under the U.S. Constitution.

1878   California Senator Aaron Sargent introduces bill calling for separate woman suffrage amendment to the U.S. Constitution (eventually the Nineteenth).

1888   First International Congress of Women, Washington, D.C.

1890   National and American Woman Suffrage Associations combine as National American Woman Suffrage Association. Wyoming enters the Union as the first woman suffrage state.

1893   Voters of Colorado pass woman suffrage amendment to state constitution. New Zealand becomes the first woman suffrage country.

1896   Voters of Idaho pass woman suffrage amendment to state constitution. First California woman suffrage referendum fails. National Association of Colored Women founded. Utah enters the Union with woman suffrage.

1903   Militant Women's Social and Political Union formed in England.

1906	International Woman Suffrage Association formed.
1907	Equality League of Self-Supporting Women organized in New York City to recruit working women.
1910	Voters of Washington pass woman suffrage amendment to state constitution.
1911	Voters of California pass woman suffrage amendment to state constitution; now there are six "suffrage states." First major parade held in New York City.
1912	Kansas, Arizona, Oregon adopt woman suffrage amendments.
1913	Militant Congressional Union formed; eight thousand women march in Washington, D.C. Alpha Suffrage Club formed by Ida B. Wells-Barnett for African-American women in Chicago. Law passed giving Illinois women "presidential suffrage," the right to vote for electors in presidential elections.
1915	First New York State woman suffrage referendum defeated; also defeats in Massachusetts, Pennsylvania, and New Jersey.
1916	Congressional Union becomes Woman's Party; organizes women of the "suffrage states" to vote against Wilson for president.
1917	United States enters World War I. In second referendum, voters of New York pass state woman suffrage amendment. Woman's Party begins demonstrations.
1918	U.S. House of Representatives passes Nineteenth Amendment.
1919	Woman's Party revives civil disobedience, arrests, and force feeding. U.S. Senate passes Nineteenth Amendment.
1920	Nineteenth Amendment is ratified.

Woman Suffrage Collections at the Huntington Library

Of all of the reforms that came out of the nineteenth century, woman suffrage has the longest history. It took women seventy-five years, and several generations of activists, to convince men of the efficacy of allowing women the right to vote. The long struggle for suffrage, and the generations of women and men who fought for and against it, are admirably represented in the collections at the Huntington Library.

The core of the woman suffrage collections at the Huntington is formed by the Susan B. Anthony Memorial Collections assembled by Alice Park and Una Winter. Composed of the papers of Anthony and other suffragists, the Memorial Collections were given to the library over a period of several decades beginning in the late 1940s. However, these are by no means the only collections which touch on the subject of woman suffrage. Below is a list of the major manuscript and ephemeral collections at the Huntington, both pro- and anti-suffrage, which document the woman suffrage movement.

Anthony Family Collection. 162 pieces, 1844–1945.
Susan B. Anthony (1820–1906), one of the founders of the suffrage movement, was also involved in the abolition and temperance movements. This collection covers Anthony's family affairs and woman suffrage activities, as well as her ideas about populism, racism, and religion. Anthony's travels to the West are also covered.

Burdette, Clara (Bradley). 50,000 pieces, 1843–1954.
The papers of Clara (Bradley) Burdette (1855–1954) document the life and activities of this Southern California social, business, and philanthropic leader. Burdette was primarily involved with the women's club movement (she founded the California Federation of Women's Clubs in 1900). As the Burdette Collection illustrates, such clubs played an important role in disseminating the suffrage movement's message.

Colby, Clara (Bewick). 237 pieces, 1882–1914.
Clara Colby (1846–1916) was active in the woman suffrage movement. Her papers, presented to the library by the Susan B. Anthony Memorial Committee in 1956, document Colby's woman suffrage activism in the West, as well as her contributions as editor of the *Woman's Tribune* in the 1880s and 1890s. There are many letters between Colby and Susan B. Anthony.

Fall, Albert Bacon. 55,000 pieces, 1887–1941.
The issue of woman suffrage was just one of many of interest to Albert B. Fall (1861–1944), senator from New Mexico and secretary of the interior under President Harding. The collection contains numerous letters between Fall, who was pro-suffrage, and members of various suffrage groups in New Mexico.

Harbert, Elizabeth Morrison (Boynton). 9,400 pieces, 1863–1925.
Elizabeth Harbert (1843–1925) was a feminist, suffragist, and lecturer. She came to suffrage from the temperance movement. Harbert was active with the National Woman Suffrage Association. In her role as editor of the "Woman's Kingdom" department of the Chicago *Inter Ocean* newspaper she corresponded with suffragists all over the West from the 1880s through the 1910s. She and her family moved to Pasadena in 1906.

Harper, Ida (Husted). 235 pieces, 1841–1919.
Publicity was integral to the dissemination of the philosophy of the suffrage movement. Ida (Husted) Harper (1851–1931) was in charge of the publicity department for the National American Woman Suffrage Association and was chosen by Susan B. Anthony to be her biographer. The Harper Collection includes much Anthony correspondence, as well as materials from Mrs. Harper's own suffrage activism.

Janin, Violet (Blair). 2007 pieces, c. 1860–1930.
Part of the larger Janin Family Collection, the papers of Violet (Blair) Janin represent the other side of the suffrage movement: those women who lobbied against women winning the right to vote. Janin, a Washington, D.C., socialite, was active with the Colonial Dames and Daughters of the American Revolution. She was also a member of the National Society Opposed to Woman Suffrage, and her diaries and letters portray the antis point of view.

Levien, Sonya. 1,280 pieces, 1908–1962.
Sonya Levien (1888?–1960) is best known as an Academy Award winning screen writer. Her award came for the screenplay *Interrupted Melody* (1955). The majority of the Levien Collection is comprised of her screenplays, but a group of papers relating to woman suffrage, including the movement's official journal, the *Woman's Journal,* can also be found.

Park, Alice (Locke). 795 pieces, 1798–1953.
Alice (Locke) Park (1861–c. 1950), was a Palo Alto journalist, feminist, pacifist, and socialite. The suffrage movement's unofficial historian, she along with Una Winter was responsible for bringing together the Susan B. Anthony Memorial Collections, of which her own papers are a part. Park was active in both national and international organizations promoting various progressive reforms, with women's rights always primary. The collection has much material on her world travels.

Severance, Caroline Maria (Seymour). 8,400 pieces, 1875–1919.
Often considered "the mother of clubs," Caroline Severance (1820–1914) was responsible for founding such Los Angeles organizations as the Friday Morning Club and Ebell Club. As this large collection proves, her interests were extremely wide, ranging from socialism to vegetarianism. She was deeply involved in woman suffrage in California, where she exerted a great deal of influence.

Strong, Harriet Williams (Russell). 1,072 pieces, 1815–1939.
Harriet Strong (1844–1926) can best be described as an agriculturalist, businesswoman, and civic leader. Perhaps because of her agricultural activities, a non-traditional role for a woman, Strong became interested in the issue of women's rights. The collection contains a number of items relating to woman suffrage, including an article called "Rights of Property and Rights of Persons," written in 1915.

Susan B. Anthony Memorial Collection. c. 1,000 pieces, 1850–1945.
Led by Alice Park and Una Winter, the Susan B. Anthony Memorial Committee collected a wide variety of ephemera, including scrapbooks, pamphlets and broadsides, photographs, postcards, posters, and buttons, among many other items relating to the campaign for woman suffrage, both in the United States and abroad. The collection includes biographical material on numerous suffrage leaders and materials from suffrage movements in every state.

Winter, Una (Richardson). 440 pieces, 1895–1954.
Una Winter (1872–1956) was director of the Susan B. Anthony Memorial Committee of California. Her feminist activism centered on women's history.

This collection contains correspondence about Winter's efforts in connection with the project, the feminist movement in the 1930s, and the National Woman's Party.

Wood, Charles Erskine Scott. Approximately 30,000 pieces, 1846–1974.

This large collection includes extensive correspondence between Sara Bard Field (1882–1974) and numerous suffragists and radical women in the early twentieth century. Field was an artist, poet, and bohemian and very active as a militant suffragist with the Woman's Party. The collection includes materials on her 1915 cross-country trip on behalf on the Nineteenth Amendment.

Suggested Reading

Barry, Kathleen. *Susan B. Anthony: A Biography of a Singular Feminist.* New York: Ballantine, 1988.

Buechler, Steven M. *Women's Movements in the United States: Woman Suffrage, Equal Rights, and Beyond.* New Brunswick: Rutgers University Press, 1990.

Camhi, Jane Jerome. *Women Against Women: American Anti-Suffragism, 1880-1920.* Brooklyn, N.Y.: Carlson Pub., 1994.

DuBois, Ellen. *Feminism and Suffrage: The Emergence of an Independent Women's Movement in America, 1848-1869.* Ithaca: Cornell University Press, 1978.

——, editor. *The Elizabeth Cady Stanton-Susan B. Anthony Reader: Correspondence, Writings, Speeches.* Boston: Northeastern University Press, 1992.

Flexner, Eleanor. *Century of Struggle: The Woman's Rights Movement in the United States.* Cambridge: Belknap Press, 1976.

Giddings, Paula. *When and Where I Enter: The Impact of Black Women on Race and Sex in America.* New York: Bantam, 1985.

Meyers, Madeleine, editor. *Forward into Light: The Struggle for Woman's Suffrage.* Lowell, Mass.: Discovery Enterprises, 1994.

Scott, Anne Firor and Andrew N. Scott. *One Half the People: The Fight for Woman Suffrage.* Urbana: University of Illinois Press, 1982.

Sheppard, Alice. *Cartooning for Suffrage.* Albuquerque: University of New Mexico Press, 1993.

Sherr, Lynn. *Failure is Impossible: Susan B. Anthony in her Own Words.* New York: Times Books, Random House, 1995.

Stanton, Elizabeth Cady. *Eighty Years and More: Reminiscences, 1815-1898.* Boston: Northeastern University Press, 1991.

Stevens, Doris. *Jailed for Freedom.* Troutdale, Ore.: NewSage Press, 1996.

Wheeler, Marjorie Spruill, editor. *One Woman One Vote: Rediscovering the Woman Suffrage Movement.* Troutdale, Ore.: NewSage Press, 1995.

Index